Trees

Trace Taylor   Gina Cline

This is a tree.

These are all trees.

Some trees are little.

Some trees are big.

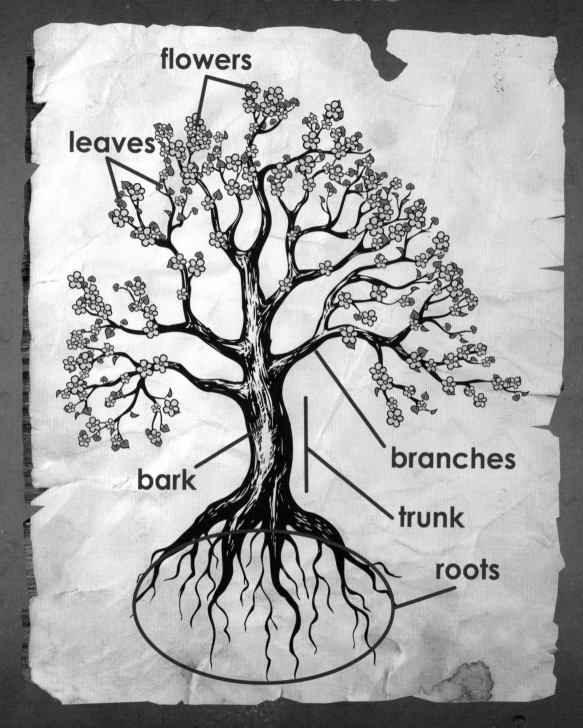

These are the parts of a tree.

All trees have roots.
The roots go into the ground.

Many trees have roots you can't see.
The roots are under the ground.

Some trees have roots you can see.

9

Roots are like feet.
Roots help a tree stand up.

If the tree didn't have roots,
it would fall down.

When it rains, water goes
down into the ground.

The roots take the water from the ground to the rest of the tree.

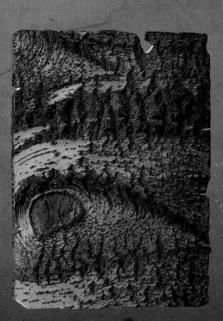

Trees have bark.

Bark is like skin for a tree.
It keeps the tree safe.

All trees have leaves.
Some leaves look like this.

Some leaves look like this.

O_2

chlorophyll

$C_6H_{12}O_6$

CO_2

Leaves turn light from the sun into food for the rest of the tree.

Leaves make clean air for us to breathe.

H_2O

Tree Life Cycle

All trees have seeds.
All of these are tree seeds.

seeds

Some trees make fruit.
There are seeds in the fruit.

Some trees make nuts.
There is one seed in each nut.

seeds

Some trees make cones.
There are seeds in the cones.

The seeds fall on the ground. A new tree will come out of the seed.

Why We Need Trees

Animals need trees. Many animals live in trees. Animals eat the seeds, nuts, fruits, leaves, and bark of trees.

People need trees. We eat the fruits and nuts trees make.

We breathe the clean air trees make.

We make houses out of trees.

We make all of these out of trees.

To make all of these things we
have to cut down the trees.

When we cut down trees, we need to plant new ones. Let's make sure we don't run out of trees.

Use words you know to read new words!

see	eat
seed	leaves
need	breathe
tree	clean
car	out
part	house
parts	houses
bark	ground